Exploring the Earth

with John Wesley Powell

by *Michael Elsohn Ross*

illustrations by *Wendy Smith*

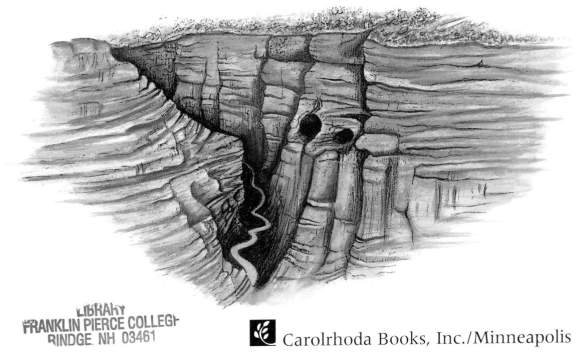

Carolrhoda Books, Inc./Minneapolis

To Alex, for your love of rocks and climbing—M.E.R.

This art is dedicated to the Earth and her preservation—W.S.

The publisher wishes to thank Ronald C. Blakey, Department of Geology at the University of Northern Arizona, for his generous assistance.

Text copyright © 2000 by Michael Elsohn Ross
Illustrations copyright © 2000 by Wendy Smith

Carolrhoda Books, Inc.
A Division of Lerner Publishing Group
241 First Avenue North, Minneapolis, MN 55401 U.S.A.

Website address: www.lernerbooks.com

LIBRARY OF CONGRESS CATALOGING-IN-PUBLICATION DATA

Ross, Michael Elsohn, 1952–
    Exploring the earth with John Wesley Powell / by Michael Elsohn Ross ;
illustrations by Wendy Smith.
        p. cm. — (Naturalist's apprentice)
    Includes bibliographical references.
    Summary: A biography of the geologist who mapped the Colorado
River and the Grand Canyon. Includes related activities.
    ISBN 1–57505–254–7
    1. Powell, John Wesley, 1834–1902—Juvenile literature.
2. Colorado River (Colo.–Mexico)—Discovery and exploration—Juvenile
literature. 3. Explorers—United States—Biography—Juvenile
literature. 4. Grand Canyon (Ariz.)—Discovery and exploration—
Juvenile literature. 5. West (U.S.)—Discovery and exploration—
Juvenile literature. 6. Geology—Study and teaching—Activity
programs—Juvenile literature. [1. Powell, John Wesley, 1834–1902.
2. Explorers. 3. Geologists. 4. Colorado River (Colo.–Mexico)—
Discovery and exploration. 5. Grand Canyon (Ariz.)—Discovery and
exploration. 6. West (U.S.)—Discovery and exploration.]
I. Smith, Wendy, ill. II. Title. III. Series: Ross, Michael
Elsohn, 1952–   Naturalist's apprentice.
F788.R67   2000
917.91'3044—dc21   99-19488

Manufactured in the United States of America
1 2 3 4 5 6 – JR – 05 04 03 02 01 00

Contents

4

Chapter 1
Listening to the Earth

Pick me up," begs a sparkly pebble. "Climb me," calls a steep hill. Do you listen to the earth? Even though the land doesn't really talk, every stone, mound of soil, and rocky ridge has a story to tell. Every mountain and valley has a history written in the language of the earth. Do you want to understand the voices of the land? Would you like to discover the mysteries of the very ground beneath your feet? Can you see yourself becoming a daring earth explorer?

In 1842, eight-year-old John Wesley Powell took his first steps toward becoming a **geologist,** a scientist who studies the earth. That year, Wes had an important encounter with rocks at school, but he wasn't studying them—he was ducking them. The rocks Wes ducked were thrown by a group of boys who didn't like him or anyone else in his family. In fact, there was a lot of hate swirling through the little town of Jackson, Ohio. Like many pioneer towns, Jackson was home to people with different ideas of freedom. Some settlers thought it was fine to own slaves. Others, called abolitionists, said slavery was wrong and should end.

Wes's parents, Joseph and Mary Dean Powell, were abolitionists. They had come to the United States from England in 1830. For a few years, they moved from place to place in New York. Wes, their third child, was born in Mount Morris on March 24, 1834. The Powells finally settled their growing family in Jackson, Ohio, in 1838. Within a few years, the family included eight children.

Although Joseph Powell was a tailor by trade, he was also a minister. The Reverend Powell had come to Jackson to preach the teachings of an Englishman named John Wesley. (Wes was named for this religious leader.) Calling themselves Methodists, Wesley's followers taught that slavery and drinking alcohol were wrong and should be stopped. These were not safe things to say in a town like Jackson, where a lot of people drank heavily and slavery had many supporters. Some people were outraged by Joseph Powell's words. At school, the sons of these angry settlers picked on Wes. When the boys started throwing rocks at Wes, Joseph and Mary decided to keep him out of school.

Joseph Powell

Luckily for Wes, this wasn't the end of his learning. On the contrary, it was the beginning of his career as a **naturalist,** a person who studies nature. When Wes stopped going to school, "Big George" Crookham, a fellow abolitionist and local naturalist, offered to become his teacher. Big George's nickname came from his size—he weighed more than three hundred pounds—but he was also vast in knowledge. He had a large collection of plants, animals, rocks, and artifacts such as Native American arrowheads.

Mary Dean Powell

He had a library and museum. And he had a school for grown men who wanted to keep learning. Wes became Crookham's youngest student and soon began to learn the language of the hills.

Wes already knew how to read. His mother, Mary, had taught Wes and her other children to read the Bible. She encouraged them to seek knowledge. As a result, Wes sparkled with curiosity and wonder. He listened carefully to his new teacher. Big George read him books that many would consider too difficult for such a young lad, but Wes was quick to understand new ideas.

Discussing books was fun, but tromping through the countryside was even better. In the wild classroom of the outdoors, Crookham taught Wes the basics of geology and archaeology—the study of the remains of ancient cultures—as well as other sciences. Dr. William Mather, Ohio's first state geologist, often came with Crookham and Wes. Together they hunted for rocks. They explored nearby Salt Creek and examined a coal deposit. They investigated rock quarries and prehistoric earth mounds.

Big George taught Wes how to explore like a scientist. Wes learned how to take careful notes and to identify rocks. Better yet, he discovered the importance of asking questions about the earth. What kind of rocks are found in a streambed? How is land shaped into hills and valleys?

Can you picture a school without walls? Can you imagine being the apprentice of two great naturalists? Wes was in heaven! He was learning from reading books, but he was also discovering how to read the earth itself.

Geo-Scout

Do you want to learn how to read the earth like John Wesley Powell? You can start by becoming a geo-scout. To be one, all you have to do is explore. Be sure to take along a scouting buddy or two like Wes did.

Supplies
✔ a notebook and pen

What to Do
✔ Prowl your neighborhood for pebbles, stones, and boulders. What colors and textures can you spot?

✔ If you live in a city, take a look at rocks in a local park, or check out the rocks used in buildings.

✔ If you live in the country, examine hills and creek beds.

✔ Tune in to the ups and downs as you cruise your neighborhood. Make a mental map of hills, valleys, and bluffs.

✔ Ask questions. Why is this hill flat on top? Why are these rocks smooth and round? How did the valley form? Jot down your questions as you explore. The more questions you ask, the sooner you'll begin to understand the language of the land.

Rock Basics

There are thousands of different types of rocks. Each type of rock is made up of a unique combination of natural solid substances called **minerals**. Rocks can be divided into three main groups: **igneous, sedimentary,** and **metamorphic.**

Igneous rocks are formed by **magma,** a very hot liquid rock found deep within the earth. When magma moves up toward the earth's surface and cools, igneous rocks are formed. Magma that cools slowly underground forms igneous rocks such as granite and peridotite. When magma erupts onto or just below the earth's surface, it cools quickly, forming igneous rocks such as obsidian, pumice, and basalt.

Sedimentary rocks are made up of sediment—tiny pieces of rocks, shells, and plants that have been broken down by wind and water. When layers of sediment are squeezed together beneath the ocean or heavy rocks, they gradually form rocks such as limestone, sandstone, and shale. Sedimentary rocks are often easy to identify because the sediment layers are usually visible.

Metamorphic rocks are rocks that have been changed by heat, pressure, or other forces. For example, heat and pressure can turn granite into a rock called gneiss.

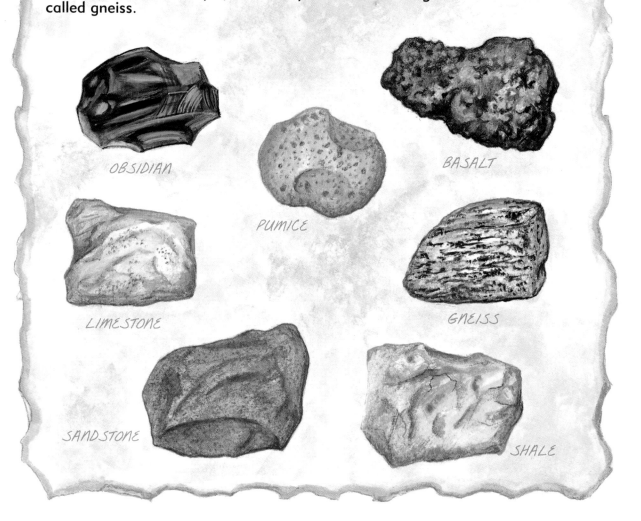

OBSIDIAN

PUMICE

BASALT

LIMESTONE

GNEISS

SANDSTONE

SHALE

Finding a Mentor

Do you know any friends or neighbors who are crazy about rocks and curious about the earth? Like Wes, you can trail along with people who are interested in learning about the earth's history. Check your community paper for notices about rock or hiking clubs. Ask your folks if they know anyone who studies geology. Perhaps an earth science teacher at the local high school can answer some of your questions, too.

Wes also learned from Crookham about being true to one's beliefs. One day, while exploring Salt Creek, they went to a remote area where Wes had never been. There, in caves high above the water, Big George introduced Wes to three men who had run away from enslavement in the South. The men were following the Underground Railroad, a secret trail north to freedom in Canada. The caves were a "station" where runaways could get food, rest, and directions. Big George wasn't just talking about stopping slavery. He was actually helping slaves follow the road to freedom—very dangerous work.

By 1844, proslavery settlers had become more and more violent. One day, a mob tried to attack Big George, Dr. Mather, and Wes's father as they walked down the street with a professor who had come to Jackson to speak against slavery. They escaped, but a few days later Crookham's school and laboratory were burned down. Gone were Big George's marvelous nature collections, notes, journals, and most of his books. Discouraged, he gave up all his students except for young Wes.

When Wes was twelve, the Reverend Powell decided to move west once again, to Wisconsin. He was drawn by cheap land and the prospect of preaching in the area's new settlements. So in 1846, Wes said good-bye to Big George Crookham and hello to his new home in South Grove, Wisconsin. Joseph, Mary, and their eight children settled on a farm with woods, meadows, and a brook brimming with trout. To Wes, the farm looked like much more fun than their home in Jackson.

By this time, Wes's parents considered him educated enough and old enough to take on the responsibility of running the farm. With tailoring and preaching to do, Joseph Powell had little time for farm work. So it was up to Wes, age twelve, and Bram, age eleven, to care for the family's two cows, four hogs, four sheep, and many chickens. They also tended the fruit trees, vegetable garden, small vineyard, and wheat fields. For hard work such as plowing and clearing trees, extra help was hired. But for the most part, the boys were on their own. Wes and Bram worked hard, grew strong, and played little.

In May of 1847, an unusual event occurred on the Powell farm. A group of Winnebago Indians camped about a mile from the house. The Powells learned that their land had once been part of the Winnebagos' hunting grounds. The government had purchased it from the Indians so that people like the Powells could settle there. This was Wes's first encounter with Native Americans, and he was fascinated. He wanted to find out about the Winnebagos' customs and language. He watched them dance, hunt, and play games. His time with these friendly, peaceful visitors marked the beginning of a lifelong fascination with the native peoples of North America— and with **ethnology,** the study of different cultures.

Like most other farm boys, Wes worked hard all day, but he also studied hard at night. He thought often of Big George Crookham and his nature collections. As Wes worked on the farm, he discovered Winnebago artifacts, so he started his own little museum. At the end of the workday, he also collected and tried to identify wildflowers and insects.

One day, while taking grain to market, Wes met William Wheeler, a young man who read books as his oxcart rolled along. Wes thought this was a great idea, so he began reading on his trips, too. As the two met on other trips, they shared their enthusiasm for books. William was twenty-one—five years older than Wes—and he encouraged Wes to go to college. He even thought that there was money to be made studying sciences such as geology.

Choosing a Field Guide

In John Wesley Powell's time, few geology books were available. Field guides to minerals and geologic features didn't exist in the 1840s, but you can find many books to choose from on the bookstore or library shelf. With a helpful field guide, you can educate yourself just as young Wes did. Try to pick a guide that has the following features:

✔ The Full Deck
Using a guide that covers only the common rocks and minerals is like playing cards without a full deck. The more rocks and geologic details your field guide covers, the more likely you'll be to find information about the less common features you encounter.

✔ Handy Helper
Pick a field guide that is simple to use. A guide with pictures and descriptions together on one page is usually easiest to work with.

✔ Lighter than Rocks
A guide doesn't need to be boulder sized to be useful. In fact, the more compact a field guide is, the more likely you'll be to take it along in your pocket or backpack the next time you venture out on a geologic expedition. An encyclopedia of geology might be packed with information, but it's a load to carry.

When Wes invited William Wheeler to meet his family, they were impressed—especially Wes's older sister Mary. Another sister, Martha, had met an intelligent, interesting man named John Davis. Within a year, Mary wed William and Martha married John. Wes had two well-educated brothers-in-law. He looked up to them and hoped that he could someday go to college, too.

First, though, Wes needed to finish studying the basics. By October of 1850, Bram was old enough to manage the farm, so Wes headed toward the nearest school, in Janesville, Wisconsin. He found a job as a hired hand on a farm near the town. He worked mornings and evenings and attended school during the day. But after only one term, Wes's father asked him to come home. He needed Wes's help to start up the family's new farm in Illinois. In return, the Reverend Powell offered to pay for Wes to go to college—if Wes would study to become a minister.

Wes wanted to become a scientist, not a minister. But he felt he had to help his family, and help he did. He cleared and plowed land, then planted, harvested, and threshed the wheat crop. The crop turned out well, so Wes got ready to leave home once again. Science still interested him, but his father thought the study of science was not a worthy pursuit. It was the ministry or nothing. Upset, Wes refused his father's offer. He would find a job teaching school and pay for college himself.

Eighteen-year-old Wes left the farm and walked thirty miles over frozen, bumpy roads, braving bitterly cold winds. Finally, he reached Jefferson County, Wisconsin. This area was filling up with new settlers, and Wes had guessed that they would need teachers. He was right. Within a day, he found a job teaching in a one-room stone schoolhouse. Some of his students were as old as he was. He had to work hard to keep ahead of a few of them, while others could barely read.

Wes kept learning, too. He taught himself advanced grammar and math and continued his geology studies. He read whatever he could find on rocks and the earth. Soon he started to give evening lectures to his older students on geography, geology, and history.

In 1853, a new college called the Illinois Institute opened in Wheaton, Illinois. The Reverend Powell had been elected a trustee and had moved the family to a small farm nearby. He encouraged Wes to attend the institute. Excited, Wes quit his teaching job and returned home. To his great disappointment, he discovered the school offered nothing that he couldn't teach himself.

Wes went back to teaching, this time near Decatur, Illinois. Again he taught an evening class in addition to his regular ones—only this time, he created a singing geography lesson. Wes's students chanted the state capitals and sang the names of Europe's mountains to a popular tune. Few students forgot what Wes taught them. He was not only gaining knowledge of geology, but also learning how to share his passion for studying the earth. Best of all, he was following his own heart.

MONT BLANC, ALPS

Emma Dean

Chapter 2
Collecting Fever

During the next few years, Wes moved from town to town. Though he continued to teach and study, his real passion was adding to his collection of rocks, plants, and animals. In 1855, he took off on his first long expedition, a rowboat trip up the Mississippi River to St. Paul, in the Minnesota Territory. His aim was to collect the shells of mollusks—clams, mussels, and other shellfish. He carried almost nothing but a little money, a notebook, and pencils. Even the mollusks he collected were mailed back to Wheaton.

After reaching St. Paul, Wes traveled across Wisconsin and Michigan to collect shells. Along the way, he visited an aunt, uncle, and cousins whom he had never met before. One cousin, Emma Dean, captivated Wes. She was beautiful, and she loved to hear him talk about his adventures. And he loved to tell her about them.

Wes spent the next few years going to school, teaching, and making river trips. Like his father, he was possessed by an urge to wander. He collected minerals in the Iron Mountain region of Missouri and searched for shells along the Great Lakes. He often ran out of money and had to find a job to pay his way home. One time, he even had to sell his watch. Before long, Wes had gathered a huge natural collection: almost six thousand pressed plants, a large assortment of mollusk shells, and a hefty supply of rocks.

The Well-Equipped Earth Explorer

Geologists use a variety of tools as they explore the land. A magnifying lens is helpful for looking closely at rocks. Notebooks are handy for jotting down observations and questions. A rock hammer works well for chipping away rock samples (be sure to wear safety goggles). To become a well-equipped earth scientist, supply yourself with the materials listed below.

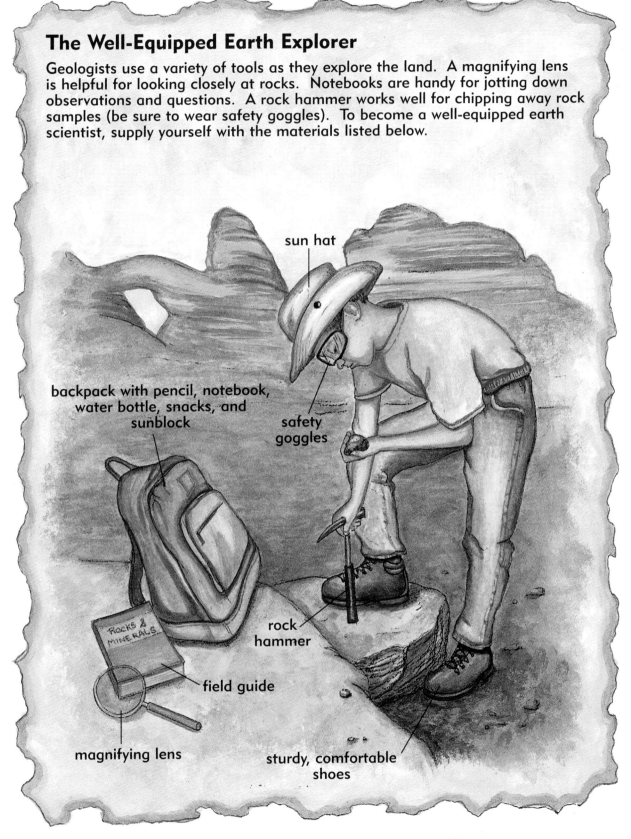

sun hat

backpack with pencil, notebook, water bottle, snacks, and sunblock

safety goggles

rock hammer

ROCKS & MINERALS

field guide

magnifying lens

sturdy, comfortable shoes

Making a Rock Collection

You can go on a rock hunt in your neighborhood or beyond. Be sure to avoid collecting rocks from local, state, or national parks, and always ask permission before taking rocks from other places.

Supplies

- ✔ rock hammer
- ✔ safety goggles
- ✔ field guide
- ✔ pencil or pen
- ✔ newspaper squares (about 6 inches across)
- ✔ bag or pack for collecting
- ✔ empty egg cartons
- ✔ masking tape

What to Do

- ✔ Look for rocks of different shapes, colors, and textures. To chip a sample from a large rock, use your rock hammer—just make sure to put on safety goggles.

- ✔ Try to identify the rocks using a field guide. Can you tell whether your rocks are igneous, sedimentary, or metamorphic?

- ✔ As you collect each rock, jot down on a sheet of newspaper where it was found. Then use the newspaper to wrap the rock.

- ✔ When you get home, place your rocks in egg cartons for storage. Use a piece of tape to label the rock with its name and the location where you found it.

How to Use a Magnifying Lens

With a magnifying lens, you can clearly see a rock's colors, textures, and patterns. You can also see its crystals, small particles that make up most minerals. To become an expert at eyeing rocks through a lens, follow these tips:

- ✔ Hold the lens up in front of one eye and close the other. If you have trouble keeping one eye closed, use your finger to hold the lid shut.

- ✔ Look closely at a rock. If it looks blurry, try moving closer, still holding the lens in front of your eye. What patterns and colors does the close-up show?

In 1858, Wes took a job as a teacher in Hennepin, Illinois, along the bluffs of the Illinois River. He was fascinated by the area's geology. The countryside was covered with deposits of gravel and sand that Wes recognized as leftovers of **glaciers**—huge, slowly moving sheets of ice—that had once covered the region. Wes knew that he could figure out the past movements of these glaciers by studying their deposits. He took careful notes on all the glacial tracks he encountered. He observed how the soil changed and how vegetation grew along the deposits. Wes was no longer just collecting—he was trying to figure out the past. He was becoming an earth detective!

Glacial Glossary

As glaciers flow down valleys and across plains, the ice picks up rocks, soil, and other materials. When a glacier melts, the materials frozen in the ice are dropped on the land. These glacial leftovers form distinctive features that remain long after a glacier disappears.

drumlin: a smooth, egg-shaped hill made of glacial deposits

kettle: a hole created when large blocks of buried ice melt. Kettles sometimes form lakes or ponds.

erratic: a boulder that has been carried by a glacier and dropped in a new area

moraine: a ridge or mound of boulders, sand, gravel, and clay

esker: a long, snakelike ridge of material deposited by a stream that flows within or under a glacier

outwash plain: a broad, flat, fan-shaped deposit of fine sand or gravel, left by melting ice

Visiting a Glacial Landscape

Like Wes, you can search for evidence of past glaciers in your neighborhood. Check out the map to determine if your home is in a region where glaciers once existed. If so, look for glacial features in your local landscape.

No matter where you live, you can observe models of typical glacial landscapes by visiting the nearest golf course—or even watching golf on television. (Before going to your local course, call to ask the manager for permission to take a tour.) Golf courses are replicas of the glaciated landscape of Scotland, where golf was invented. Sand traps are piles of glacial outwash. Water traps are modeled on the ponds formed by kettles. The greens are grassy areas where fine particles of soil called silt were deposited. The tree hazards mimic the groves of trees that grow atop eskers or moraines, where rich soil makes conditions good for growth.

Glaciers once covered the parts of North America that are colored white.

Alaska U.S.

CANADA

Hudson Bay

UNITED STATES

MEXICO

While Wes was traveling, he frequently exchanged letters with his cousin Emma. He often visited her in Detroit, too. As before, she was thrilled by the tales Wes told about his explorations. In fact, she wished that she could join him. Their parents grew worried. What if Wes and Emma, first cousins, wanted to get married? But Wes wasn't ready to marry. Though he had a job, he spent every penny on his expeditions. For the time being, Wes Powell would rather collect rocks than settle down with a wife.

Chapter 3
Journey into War

In the spring of 1861, Wes's life—and the lives of everyone else in the United States—took a dramatic turn. For years, tension had been growing between the slaveowners of the South and the abolitionists of the North. In April, the Civil War began. Wes decided to act on his abolitionist beliefs by joining the North's Union army. He knew that his knowledge of geography and mapping would come in handy. He also prepared himself by studying military tactics and engineering, especially bridge building.

By June, Wes had been promoted to second lieutenant. His regiment was stationed in Cape Girardeau, Missouri, along the banks of the Mississippi. Only a few years earlier, Wes had traveled up and down the river to study nature. This time, he was preparing to help defend a town against Confederate, or Southern, troops. General Ulysses S. Grant put Wes in charge of forty men and six cannons. As the men spent long days waiting for action, they became experts at bowling with thirty-two-pound cannonballs.

In November, General Grant gave Wes permission to travel to Detroit to marry Emma. (Wes and Emma's parents had decided to let the marriage take place.) They were married on November 28, and after a brief visit with Wes's parents, the two returned to Cape Girardeau. They weren't hunting for rocks or shells, but Emma had finally gotten her wish to join Wes on his adventures.

Back at the fort, Wes and his soldiers trained endlessly. In the middle of March, they were moved up the river. Then, in early April, a large force of Confederate troops attacked the Union encampment. Wes quickly moved his guns and troops to the battlefront. As he gave the signal to fire, a bullet struck his right arm.

Wes was sent to a nearby hospital, where Emma met him. The wound was so bad that the doctor had to cut off part of the arm.

Wes in uniform

When Wes awoke from his surgery, he found only a bandaged stump where his lower arm had been. It was a strange sensation. Wes could "feel" his hand and lower arm, even though they were gone. Fortunately, Emma was there to nurse him back to health.

After a few months, Wes left the hospital and was sent to Illinois to recruit new soldiers. Though his stump throbbed with pain, he kept working. In February of 1863, he was ordered to return to his men. After marching for weeks, the troops surrounded the Confederate town of Vicksburg, Mississippi. There, they spent forty days preparing for battle. During his short periods of rest, Wes sketched the river and examined the area's rocks and landforms.

Landform Basics

As you've probably noticed, the earth's landscape is as varied as its people. Check out this guide to common landforms, then see which ones you can discover in your own neighborhood.

BUTTE

VALLEY

CLIFF

MESA

CANYON

SPIT

PLAIN

DUNE

MOUNTAIN

Traveling on a Pencil

What does the land around you look like? Are there sand dunes, plains, cliffs, valleys, or mesas? Even if you live in a city, your neighborhood has its own landforms. Like John Wesley Powell, you can find out about the local landscape by traveling across it with a pencil.

Supplies
✔ paper
✔ pencil

What to Do
✔ Settle yourself in a spot where you have a good view of the land. Sketch the ups and downs, then compare them to the landforms in the drawings on page 21.

✔ What landforms did you notice as you traveled with your pencil? Did you discover any that you had never paid attention to before?

On the evening of July 3, 1863, Wes received orders to begin shooting at daybreak. But the fighting never started. The next morning, a hundred white flags, signaling surrender, waved from the walls of Vicksburg. The battle was over, but Wes's pain continued. The stump of his arm ached continually. Wes had to have an operation to remove sensitive nerves. While he was recovering, he got word that he had been promoted to the rank of major.

Wes served in the army for another long, hard year and a half. He witnessed bloody battles, and his younger brother Walter was captured and imprisoned by the Confederates. Wes was worn out. Despite the operation, his stump still hurt. He asked for a medical discharge and was released from the army in January of 1865. That March, Walter returned home from the prisoner-of-war camp where he had been held. The family was overjoyed to see him, but he was a sad sight. He was not only terribly thin but also moody and unpleasant. The war had left its mark on Wes and Walter.

Back home in Wheaton, Wes thought about his future. He wasn't sure what to do because he had so many ideas. Again his father tried to advise him. "Wes, you are a maimed man," Joseph said. "Settle down to teaching. It is a noble profession. Get this nonsense of science and adventure out of your mind."

Do you think Wes listened?

HIRASE'S VOLUTE

TIGER COWRY

RED ABALONE

Chapter 4
Down the Canyon

At first, it looked like Wes really would settle down, just as his father had suggested. He accepted a job teaching geology at Illinois Wesleyan University and moved with Emma to Bloomington. The pay was good, and the college was near the town of Normal, where the Illinois Natural History Society kept its collections. Years before, Wes had been elected as curator, or caretaker, of the society's shell collection, so he was glad to be near it again.

Wes was an enthusiastic teacher, and his classes became popular. He taught differently than other science professors. Instead of boring his students with long lectures, Wes showed them how to do real science. They performed chemical experiments to discover the characteristics of rocks. They roamed prairies, streams, and woods, studying plants, animals, and the earth.

Besides teaching, Wes lectured in towns across the countryside about the practical value of science. He argued that science could prepare people for the difficult problems of the times, such as the diseases and pests that threatened farmers' crops. Wes's listeners were amazed by his memory as he rattled off facts and figures. His soft, clear voice and wild red hair made a strong impression, too.

Life was good, but it was too quiet. The old thirst for adventure was like a dry scratch in Wes's throat. He began to read about the mountains and deserts of the West. Many of them were unmapped, and little was known about the area's geology.

When Wes told Emma he wanted to explore the West, she agreed that he should follow his heart. Immediately Wes began rearranging his life. First he persuaded the leadership of the Illinois Natural History Society to appoint him curator of the society's entire museum. Then he arranged an expedition to the Colorado Territory to collect new items for the museum.

In the army, Wes had easily organized and commanded his men. He soon discovered that he could also put together a scientific crew with ease. Many people were interested in the land and natural resources of the West, and they knew that good maps would lead the way to settlement of the region. Wes asked for help and got it from many places. The museum gave him money. Colleges gave cash in exchange for Wes's promise to collect plants, animals, and rocks for them. Even the Smithsonian Institution in Washington, D.C., loaned him scientific instruments.

In July of 1867, Wes's group explored the rugged Colorado Rockies, collecting birds, insects, plants, and **fossils,** or the remains of once-living things preserved in rock. Wes sketched the mountains and took notes on the area's geology. Emma went along—not only to be with Wes, but also as one of the expedition's two bird experts. At the end of the month, she climbed Pikes Peak with the rest of the crew, trudging through three-foot-deep snow in a long dress made of waterproof cloth. Emma became the first woman to reach the mountain's summit.

Fossil Facts

When plants and animals die, they usually **decompose,** or break down slowly, and become part of the soil. But when the remains of living things are buried in sediment, they may become fossils instead. Over the course of millions of years, the weight of many layers of sediment can turn the remains into rock. Sometimes only the outline of the plant or animal is left behind in the rock, and even a trace as small as a footprint can become a fossil. Because of the way fossils are formed, they are usually found in sedimentary rocks.

Fossil Find

The study of fossils is called paleontology. Fossils can be found in most parts of North America. Can you find any near your home?

Supplies
✔ rock hammer
✔ chisel
✔ safety goggles
✔ hard hat or helmet
✔ newspaper squares
✔ pen or pencil
✔ notebook
✔ backpack

What to Do

✔ Ask an earth science teacher, rock club leader, or museum expert if there are fossils in your area. Find out where you are allowed to collect them, and ask for permission before you start.

✔ Keep in mind a few safety tips: Take along a fossil-finding buddy, make sure an adult knows where you're going, and never climb steep cliffs to look for fossils.

✔ Fossils may be found in places where sedimentary rock is exposed. Try looking near streambeds, lakes, or oceans. Scan the rock for particles that look like plant or animal parts.

✔ If you find a fossil, carefully extract it by chiseling around it. (Be sure to put on safety goggles and a hard hat or helmet before you start to chisel.) Try to be gentle—if you hammer directly on or too close to the fossil, it may break.

✔ Wrap your fossil in newspaper labeled with the location where you found it. Keep a record of your fossil finds.

✔ To find out more about your fossils, talk to an earth science teacher or look for a fossil guide at your local library.

Months later, Wes returned home with nine hundred birds, several hundred plants, and thousands of insects and reptiles—plus boxes of rocks, minerals, and fossils. The museum trustees were so impressed that they gladly gave support for another expedition. This time, Wes wanted to explore the vast, unmapped lands of the upper Colorado River. It took him a while to get there, though. During the summer and fall of 1868, Wes's team climbed peaks to measure their elevations and collected more materials for museums. Moving westward, they soon reached the White River and built log cabins for a winter camp. Not far from the cabins lived a group of Ute (YOOT) Indians, and Wes befriended them. During the long winter nights, he learned the Utes' language, myths, and customs. Wes recorded everything he learned, and Emma added many sketches to his writings.

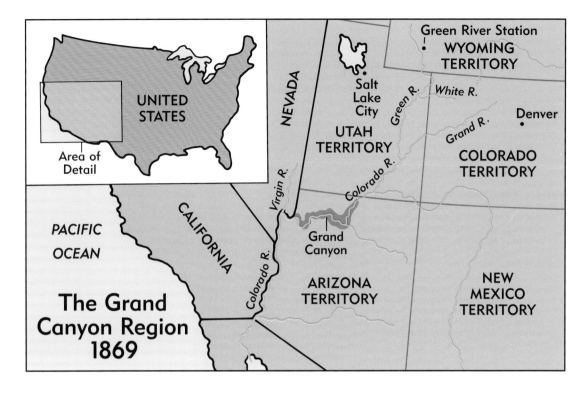

The Grand Canyon Region 1869

When spring came, the party traveled through rugged country, following the White River to its junction with the Green River. This was Wes's goal—the beginning of the Grand Canyon region. Maps of the area showed only a blank spot four hundred miles long and two hundred miles wide. Mapmakers believed that the Green River flowed into the Colorado, and there were reports that the river rushed through deep gorges, bounded by cliffs too high to climb. From the Green River junction to the Virgin River in Arizona, the river dropped one vertical mile. No other large river in the United States dropped so steeply. Would there be falls and rapids, or swift water, too dangerous to navigate?

In spite of the danger, Wes was determined to map the area and investigate its geology. He decided that the best way to explore the region was by boat. The land was too rough to travel by foot. Wes gathered all the information he could find, then went home to raise funds. He had four riverboats designed and built. The expedition's lead boat would be Wes's, and he named it the *Emma Dean* after his wife. The boats were shipped by railroad to the Green River, then loaded with provisions for ten months. Only ten men would go on this trip, and for the first time Emma would stay at home.

The journey began on May 24, 1869. For a few days, the going was easy and the scenery was eye-catching. The men floated beneath bluffs of multicolored rock layers and glimpsed faraway mountains. They spied deer and bighorn sheep on the cliffs. Soon the party entered a brilliant red canyon that they named Flaming Gorge. There, the journey got harder. They reached rapids that were so rough the men had to land and lower the boats with ropes, then climb down and start again.

Whenever the boats approached rough rapids, Wes, in the lead boat, would signal the others to land. On June 8, the last boat missed a signal, entered a series of rough rapids, and crashed into several boulders. Although the boat was destroyed, its crew was rescued. But the boat's cabin contained Wes's barometers, instruments needed to measure the elevation of the land. When the men found the remains of the cabin down the river, two volunteered for the dangerous task of salvaging what they could from the wreckage. Fortunately, they found the barometers, and the expedition continued.

A week later, the party almost lost another boat. Soon after, a fire in their camp burned up some clothes and other supplies. After traveling a few days more, Wes and a few men walked thirty miles to a trading post. They wanted to buy more food, but the trading post had little to offer, and the men couldn't get as much as they needed. Many of the crew had become concerned about the lack of food for the rest of the journey. One of the men abandoned the expedition, so the party was down to nine.

As the voyage continued, the men were rewarded by the discovery of a magical canyon where their voices echoed back and forth again and again. There, Wes and a crew member named George Bradley scaled a wall to get a look at the surrounding country. They had climbed over six hundred feet above the river when Wes became stranded on a shelf of rock. He couldn't find a way up or down. Bradley climbed to a higher ledge but couldn't reach Wes. How could Bradley help him off the shelf? Quickly Bradley stripped off his trousers and dangled them over the ledge. Wes grabbed the pants and held tight as Bradley hoisted him up.

The river trip was full of adventures like Wes's canyon climb, plus a lot of hard work. But there were also many hours of quiet observation as the boats floated along. Wes hoped to learn more about how the canyons were formed, and he carefully noted their geology as he drifted between the massive walls. He recorded the type of rock in each area and collected samples. Soon the men were carrying bags of light gray sandstone, red sandstone, polished marble, and sharp, dark shale. The crew also collected fossils and Native American artifacts.

The journey didn't get easier. Paddles were broken on rocks and had to be recarved from driftwood. One night, the party was caught in a sandstorm and had to lay low until it stopped. As the crew descended the river, they spent hours lowering their boats through surging rapids. Several times, a boat was unable to pull ashore in time and was overturned by huge waves that rose higher than the boats. Even Wes landed in the river. Luckily he was a strong swimmer, even with only one arm.

Each time a boat turned over, something else was lost. Food and equipment grew scarce, but the men still had the scientific tools they needed to figure elevations and their approximate location. One night, one of the men played with an instrument called a sextant, saying he was trying to discover the location of the nearest pie. Unfortunately, Wes and his crew were as far from pie as anyone could get.

Though they were short on comfort, the men were rewarded with grand landscapes. The canyon's rock layers were colored like a richly dyed blanket, and the crew saw incredible buttes striped in gray, pink, purple, and brown. The boats floated into calm bays below gigantic caves. Cathedral-shaped spires of rock rose taller than any built by humans. Wes marveled at towers and rock arches. He sketched the folds and dips of rock layers. He was sure he was seeing clues to the mystery of the formation of the canyons. What discoveries lay ahead?

By the time the party reached the Colorado's junction with the Paria River, Wes had learned how to read the rocks to tell if rapids lay ahead. Minerals (and the rocks they make up) vary in **hardness,** or resistance to being scratched. Soft rock can be easily scratched and broken down into small particles. When the river flowed over layers of soft rock, it wore the rock down gradually, and the river stayed quiet. Hard rock, on the other hand, resists scratching and breaking. When it does break, it creates jagged shelves and boulders. Over hard rock, the river turned into rapids.

Wes made other interesting observations. During a wild rainstorm, he watched in amazement as rivers of red sand washed over the canyon's limestone walls from the plateaus above. Wes could understand how the walls had become so well polished. It was as if someone had scoured them with fine sandpaper.

Hard Facts

In 1822, a German scientist named Friedrich Mohs developed a way to rank the hardness of minerals and rocks. Using minerals such as talc, which is very soft, and diamond, which is very hard, Mohs created a scale that measured hardness from one to ten. If you rub together two minerals or rocks of different hardness, the harder one will scratch the softer one. For example, quartz will scratch feldspar but not diamond, which is harder than quartz. Hardness is one of the characteristics geologists use to identify rocks, so knowing Mohs' scale can come in handy.

Mohs' Scale

1. TALC

6. FELDSPAR

2. GYPSUM

7. QUARTZ

3. CALCITE

8. TOPAZ

9. CORUNDUM

4. FLUORITE

5. APATITE

10. DIAMOND

Tough Times

Unlike Friedrich Mohs or other geologists, you may not have all the minerals in Mohs' scale to compare with the rocks you find. Instead, you can use common materials to create a modified Mohs' scale. Each of the materials listed below will scratch a mineral of the same or lesser hardness, but not a mineral of greater hardness. A fingernail will scratch talc (1) and gypsum (2), but not calcite (3). Ask your folks for permission to assemble some of these items and check out the hardness of the minerals and rocks in your collection.

Item	Hardness
fingernail	approximately 2.5
copper penny	approximately 3.0
glass	5.0–5.5
penknife blade	5.5–6.0
steel file	6.5–7.0

At last, John Wesley Powell and his crew reached the Grand Canyon itself. There, the walls became closer and the water swifter. The canyon's walls rose higher and higher, until they reached over a mile above the snaking Colorado. Spires and craggy pinnacles, polished by the wind and waves, jutted out along the walls and even in the riverbed itself. The shore was so narrow and rocky they had to run many rapids instead of lowering the boats.

Wes felt small and insignificant in this deep gorge. Later, he wrote about the experience, "Down these grand, gloomy depths we glide, ever listening, for the mad waters keep up their roar, ever watching, ever peering ahead, for the narrow canyon is winding and the river so closed in that we can see but a few hundred yards, and what there may be below we know not." Despite the danger, the men ran the biggest rapids without trouble, and further into the depths they went.

Beyond the Grand Canyon, the going was easier. Still, each day brought more rapids—more work to lower the boats and supplies and more gut-wrenching rides through fast water. The only food left was coffee and moldy flour for making bread. The crew were becoming tired, hungry, and uncomfortable. Wes, on the other hand, was so absorbed in his discoveries that he didn't seem to notice the discomfort of the trip or even the usual pain in the stump of his arm. On August 27, three of the men decided they were finished with river running. They would walk across the desert to the closest settlement. Wes sadly gave them some food and guns and bid them farewell.

Only six men remained—not enough to row three boats. The *Emma Dean* was in such bad shape that they left it behind. The men had to store the rock and fossil collections near the river and hope they could return to pick them up during a future expedition.

Wes in December 1869, after his expedition

And the worst rapid of all lay ahead. Still, the crew kept going. The boats were tossed like toys and filled with water, but somehow they made it through. On August 30, the Powell expedition reached a Mormon settlement at the mouth of the Virgin River. They had made it to safety! The three men who had set out across the desert were not so lucky. When Wes journeyed to Salt Lake City on his way home, he learned that the men had been killed by a group of Shivwit Indians, a usually peaceful Native American tribe. The Shivwits had mistaken Wes's men for miners who had killed a Shivwit woman.

Wes returned home and reunited with Emma. His explorations of the unknown canyon country caught the public's interest, and he became a national hero. Everyone wanted to hear about the trip. Wes shared stories of the voyage with his family, his friends, and the crowds that came to attend his lectures in Wheaton, Detroit, and Cincinnati. He told of the crew's boating adventures, described the beauty of the Grand Canyon, and explained what he had discovered about the geologic history of the region.

As Wes had journeyed past mile after mile of cliffs, pinnacles, and side canyons, he had pondered the history of the land. How had the canyon been created? How had the thousands of feet of rock layers been exposed? Floating down the river was like traveling into a great geologic book. Each layer of rock told a different story about the earth's past. Wes and his crew had sketched the rock layers they saw, collected minerals and fossils, and started to make a geologic map that showed where the different types of rock were found.

As they gathered information, Wes began to solve the mystery of the canyon's creation. He believed that the layers of rock that formed the canyon walls had been created by a process called **sedimentation**—the same process that leads to the creation of sedimentary rocks. Worn down from mountains of the past, tiny bits of rock accumulated into layers. Gradually, these layers hardened into a plateau of solid rock. But how had the plateau turned into a canyon?

In Wes's time, geologists had two very different ideas about how landforms were created and how they changed. Until the mid-1800s, most geologists believed that Earth was only about six thousand years old. They thought that mountains, valleys, and canyons were the result of sudden, huge upheavals of land. These geologists, faced with the Grand Canyon, would have probably suggested it was formed by an earthquake or similar earth movement, then filled with the waters that formed the Colorado River.

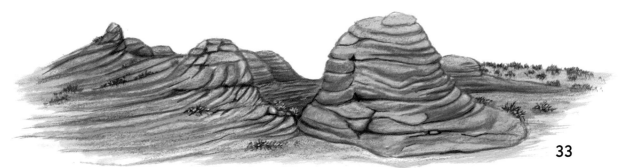

At the end of the 1700s, some geologists began to believe that Earth was much older. They found evidence that the everyday forces of nature, such as wind and rain, caused changes in the earth—sometimes very, very slowly. By the time Wes explored the Grand Canyon in 1869, more scientists had accepted this idea. And the more Wes thought about what he had seen, the more he believed that this second group of geologists had to be right. All those layers of rock couldn't have been created and exposed in just six thousand years. They must have built up slowly through sedimentation, then been exposed over millions of years by **erosion,** the gradual wearing away of rock and soil by wind and water. The Colorado River had existed long before the canyon was created, and its waters had slowly carved the canyon out of the plateau.

Wes believed that at the same time erosion was creating the canyon, another process—**uplift**—was at work. As the water flowed, the plateau had risen toward the river. Wes suggested that the river was like a saw fixed in one spot, and the plateau was like a log rising into it and being sliced. That was why the canyon was so deep. Wes couldn't explain how the plateau moved up, but the evidence he had observed made him sure that it did. He was right.

Erosion Facts

Did you know that Earth's rocks, hills, and mountains are slowly being worn down? Erosion is constantly happening in many ways, but it's such a slow process that we usually don't notice it. When water freezes in stony cracks, it expands, exerting an incredible force. Repeated freezing and thawing over time can split even large, hard boulders. When rainwater combines with gases such as sulfur dioxide or carbon dioxide, it becomes a weak acid that can slowly eat away rock. Fierce winds carry sand and gravel, creating sandstorms like those that Wes experienced. These sandstorms can slowly sculpt rock like giant sheets of sandpaper. Even plants and animals can break rocks. Roots growing in cracks slowly expand until they push rock apart. Burrowing animals dig tunnels that expose rocks to the erosive forces of water.

Wear Down a Mountain

Would you like to see erosion in action? You probably can't create a sandstorm in your backyard, but you can wear down your own mountain by following a few easy steps.

Supplies
✔ trowel
✔ shovel
✔ dirt or sand
✔ hose or watering can

What to Do

✔ Build a model mountain out of dirt or sand in a sandbox, on a beach, or in a vacant garden plot. Be sure you have permission before you start digging and sculpting. Make your mountain as big as you want.

✔ Use your watering can or hose to create a sprinkle, a drizzle, and a major rainstorm. How does the erosion change as you vary the flow of water?

✔ Notice where the sediment goes. (Try not to send it into a prize flower garden or onto the front walk!) Does the sediment create new landforms?

✔ Compare the eroded mountain with pictures of real mountains. What differences and similarities do you notice?

Since Wes's time, scientists have learned that Earth has a hard outer layer called the **crust.** The crust is made up of huge blocks of rock called plates. Forces within the earth can make the plates shift and slide, causing uplift and other large earth movements.

More than one hundred years after Wes's expedition, geologists are still learning about how the Grand Canyon was formed. Their theories are much more complex than Wes's ideas, but like Wes, many believe that sedimentation, erosion, and uplift caused much of the canyon's creation.

Wes Powell had taken not only a wild ride through a river canyon but also a journey deep into time. What other mysteries waited to be uncovered in the vast lands of the West? Wes knew there were other canyons and mountain ranges to explore. There were unknown plants and animals to collect. And Wes wanted to meet and learn more from the area's Native Americans.

Immediately after he returned home, Wes began to organize a second Colorado River expedition. This one would be two years long. He would bring better boats, and food would be stored ahead of time along the way. By May of 1871, Wes had assembled a new crew. Among them was a photographer loaded down with a large camera, glass plates, and photo-developing equipment. His supplies alone weighed more than a ton! As the boats floated down the Green River, Wes sat in a sturdy wooden chair strapped to the deck of the new *Emma Dean*.

For the most part, this trip went more smoothly than the first. Wes remembered where many of the rapids were, so he led the group cautiously. The men had life jackets, waterproof bags for gear, and improved oars, but still there were mishaps. Sometimes the river was so low they scraped bottom. At other times, the river was many feet higher than it had been in 1869, causing the boats to flip over.

Wes took several solo trips overland to explore the high plateaus and to visit Emma,

The second Emma Dean, *complete with Wes's chair strapped to the deck*

who was in Salt Lake City. She was expecting a child, and Wes found it hard to be so far away. In October, Wes left the crew while they established a winter camp in Kanab, a small Mormon community. After visiting Emma and their newborn daughter, Mary, Wes returned to camp to begin geologic explorations and to catch up on mapping. In early December, Emma and baby Mary arrived in the camp to spend the winter with Wes. Despite the cold weather and tent housing, most of the crew managed to be festive. Wes and Emma spent a lot of time in a nearby village of Ute Indians, learning about their customs and language.

Beginning the next February, the crew floated down much of the river without their leader. Wes was busy securing more funds, buying food and equipment, and exploring. In the middle of August, he rejoined the river party and floated through Marble Canyon. The river was very high due to the melting of heavy snows from the winter before, so the going was hard. At times, the men expected to be tumbled to bits by the severe rapids. During one storm, they watched the river rise fifteen feet overnight. Another time, the *Emma Dean* capsized, and Wes was plunged deep into a water-filled hole. He was wearing a life jacket, so he popped back up like a cork. The men joked that he had gone under on purpose to study the geology of the riverbed!

As the crew continued down the deep, narrow canyons, they noticed driftwood wedged high up on the walls—sometimes as high as one hundred feet. The water was surging so forcefully, and so high, that it had forced bits of wood into the rock. Could it do the same to their boats? On September 8, 1872, Wes decided to end the voyage. The next day, the men left their boats behind and walked to the nearest settlement.

Wes's second crew at the start of their 1871 expedition. Wes stands tall in the middle boat, third from the left.

Wes meets with Tau-gu, a Paiute chief, on the Virgin River in the early 1870s.

Chapter 5
Survey Days

Wes had become an experienced explorer, mapmaker, and geologist. He had also pursued his interest in ethnology through learning about the Native Americans he met. In many cases, he had won their friendship. Shivwit Indians had named him Ka-pu-rats, meaning "One Arm Off." That was what Wes was called by the many Paiutes, Utes, and Shoshones he met on his journeys. Word had spread from tribe to tribe about this energetic one-armed explorer who was so respectful of Native American ways.

Many of these native peoples were facing terrible challenges. New settlers had been moving into the western valleys, forcing out the Native Americans who lived there. In parts of Utah, Arizona, southeastern California, and southern Idaho, the Utes, Paiutes, and Shoshones were starving. When government officials learned about Wes's relationships with Native Americans, they asked him to help work out a way to resettle the western tribes.

Wes believed in the rights of all people, regardless of culture or race. But he also believed the Native Americans couldn't return to their old ways of life, because settlers from the United States couldn't be stopped from taking their land. The old ways should be remembered, but Wes also wanted Native Americans to learn to farm, so they could survive. Near ancient cliff dwellings in the canyons, Wes had seen ditches used for **irrigation**— carrying water from rivers or lakes to dry land. He had visited the agricultural Hopis and other farming tribes. These people farmed on dry land. Couldn't others do the same? Wes agreed to help the government find a new way of life for the tribes of the West.

Wes and a Ute Indian named Yan-mo in Utah's Uinta Valley

Soon Wes was traveling throughout the Colorado Basin, talking with Native American leaders and making notes on how many people were left in each tribe. He was shocked to discover how small the numbers were. Disease and starvation had killed many in just a few years. Wes reported his findings to Washington. He suggested that each Native American family be given land and tools for farming and that U.S. soldiers be removed from peaceful settlements. Unfortunately, many congressmen from western states didn't want to help Native Americans—they just wanted to get rid of them. Most of Wes's recommendations were ignored.

After Wes finished his studies of Native Americans in 1873, he, Emma, and little Mary settled into their new home in Washington, D.C., about a mile from the Smithsonian Institution. Wes continued his studies and directed a government survey, or study, of the Colorado River area. Life was busy, but he still found time to stroll with Mary through the city's parks, where they investigated flowers and admired the statues of Civil War generals Wes had served with. At the Smithsonian, he showed Mary the things he had collected on his expeditions. Whether it was a fossil or a piece of ancient pottery, Wes delighted in sharing his discoveries with his daughter.

During the next few years, Wes worked with a group of explorers, mapping parts of the Colorado Basin. He made detailed studies of the Uinta Mountains, as well as other ranges in Utah and southern Idaho. In 1874, he published a report about his Colorado River adventures. Some of the members of Wes's Grand Canyon crew were critical of this report. They said Wes hadn't told everything as it really happened and hadn't given credit to some of the crew. Although the report earned Wes some criticism, it also brought him new respect from scientists and the general public. More people than ever learned about the Grand Canyon and its history. And the name "Grand Canyon," which Wes had heard before his expeditions, stuck to the region for good. For this reason, Wes is sometimes given credit for naming the Grand Canyon.

As Wes immersed himself further in the western landscape and its peoples, he thought more and more about how human beings might best live with the land. Not all land is the same, he observed. The land of the eastern United States got plenty of water and had been farmed for centuries. The land of the West, however, was fragile and arid, or very dry. It could easily be destroyed by too many grazing animals, by logging in the high mountains, or by poor farming methods. The cliff-dwelling tribes of the Colorado Basin had learned to live on this arid land by irrigating. They understood the land and knew how to survive on it. Unless the new settlers also learned to use the land properly, it would quickly erode.

By the mid-1870s, Wes's survey was only one of many in the West. Wes suggested that Congress create a single survey that would study the geology and geography of the entire United States, providing the information the country would need to decide how to best use the land. Several important scientists agreed with Wes, and in 1879 Congress formed the United States Geological Survey (USGS).

Erosion Investigations

You've found out how to erode a mountain, but can you think of a way to keep erosion from happening? Try the ideas below and see what you can discover about keeping earth together.

Supplies
- ✔ dirt or sand
- ✔ trowel
- ✔ watering can or hose
- ✔ grass clippings, leaves, or sticks

What to Do
- ✔ Make a model mountain out of sand or dirt.

- ✔ Cover one side of the mountain with grass clippings and the other side with leaves. (If you don't have any grass clippings, try twigs, rocks, or shells.) Use a watering can or hose to erode your mountain. Which side of the mountain wears down the least?

- ✔ Cover the entire mountain with sticks, leaves, and grass clippings.

Do these materials together prevent erosion better than one alone?

- ✔ Try pouring different amounts of water on the mountain. Which material provides the best protection against a heavy downpour?

- ✔ How could your discoveries be used to help prevent erosion on a farm, ranch, or mountainside?

At the same time, Congress created the Bureau of American Ethnology to study and record the culture of Native Americans. Wes was named director of this program. An exciting and overwhelming opportunity lay ahead. There was much to learn, but the knowledge Wes sought was vanishing quickly as older Native Americans died. He soon asked ethnologists and others who worked with Native Americans for help.

After barely a year in this new job, Wes was asked to lead the USGS as well. For Wes, running the survey was a scientific fact-finding mission. The survey's job was to find out about rocks, minerals, fossils, rivers, deserts, forests, irrigation, flood control, and a whole lot more. Wes set up a chemical lab in Washington to analyze rocks. He also focused on mapping the entire United States. A big part of this task would be the making of geologic maps, which show the types of rocks in an area, and topographic maps, which use lines to show changes in elevation. Wes set up new standards for mapmaking that are still used.

Wes still believed that irrigation could turn much of the dry land of the West into farmland. He hoped that canals or pipelines could bring water to dry areas. But irrigation would be worthless if the soil in a particular area was poor. So the USGS did some serious dirty work! Wes's team gathered and categorized soil, then made soil maps. These maps showed the types of soil in an area and which lands could be farmed. Despite years of this work, however, Wes was unable to convince Congress to support irrigation of the West.

Soil Facts

Soil is made of recycled materials such as the decomposed remains of animals and plants. When rocks are worn down into tiny particles, they join the soil, too. Soil contains three main types of mineral particles. Sand grains are the largest, while clay particles are the smallest. Silt particles are smaller than sand grains but larger than clay particles. The difference in size between sand and clay is enormous. If a clay particle was as big as the period at the end of this sentence, a grain of sand would be as big as this entire page.

Dirty Survey

Like John Wesley Powell, you too can survey the soil. Here's how to do a little dirty work of your own.

Supplies
✔ teaspoon
✔ sheet of white paper
✔ magnifying lens

✔ tweezers
✔ pencil

What to Do

✔ Scoop a teaspoon of your local dirt onto a piece of paper and spread it out. Zoom in with your magnifying lens and check out the miniature terrain.

✔ Can you find particles of sand, silt, or clay? (Not all soils have all three types of particles.) The tiniest particles on your paper are probably clay. Even through a magnifying lens, clay particles will look very small. Silt particles

will be slightly larger and darker. Sand grains resemble little bits of glass.

✔ Use your tweezers to separate any large particles from the dirt. Can you spot any recycled bits of plants or animals, such as leaf bits or bug parts? Write down what you see, then invite your friends or family to help you search out more discoveries.

Wes in his office at the Bureau of Ethnology

Chapter 6
Legacy

For several years, John Wesley Powell supervised the investigation of Native American peoples and the American landscape. His network of scientists mapped, collected, developed theories, and wrote reports. Wes became a world leader in scientific studies. He was accomplishing more in a few years than most people could in a lifetime, but he was wearing himself out. Whenever the stump of his arm was bumped or jarred, sharp pains shot through it. Wes's doctors said he needed another operation. On top of this, Congress cut the survey's funds and took more control over its operations. In May of 1894, at the age of sixty, Wes retired as chief of the USGS.

Wes kept his job as director of the Bureau of Ethnology, so after recovering from his arm operation, he got back to work studying Native Americans and writing geology guides for teachers and young people. He also wrote a paper discussing the possible reasons for movements of the earth's crust and the earthquakes that result.

Though he continued to work hard, Wes was finally ready for a more relaxed life. In 1896, Emma, Mary, and Wes began to spend their summers in the small community of Haven on the coast of Maine. There Wes made friends with fishers, sea captains, and other local folk. He studied Native American shell heaps along the shore. These piles of shells held information about the lives of the coastal peoples of the past. Mixed in with the discarded shells were fragments of pottery, animal bones, and flint tools.

Most of all, Wes loved to go out on the rough sea. When the wind picked up and the water became choppy, he would don a sea captain's hat and hire a boat to take him out. He loved to feel the rain beating on his face. It wasn't exactly like the wild waters of the canyons, but perhaps it was close enough.

In late 1900, Wes traveled to Cuba and Jamaica to study the Carib and Arawak peoples. The trip exhausted him, and in the fall of 1901, he had a stroke. While he was recovering, Wes heard that President Theodore Roosevelt was interested in starting irrigation projects in the arid West. It had taken twenty-five years for Wes's ideas about irrigation to gain acceptance.

Sporting his sea captain's hat, Wes cruises off the coast of Maine with friends in 1901.

In June of 1902, a new government agency was formed to carry out irrigation projects. The following September, Wes died peacefully in his Maine bungalow. Emma lived for another twenty-two years and saw the birth of some of the conservation programs that Wes had fought so hard for. Another of his many ideas—a proposal for a national department of science—became a reality in 1950, when the National Science Foundation was established.

Like John Wesley Powell, you can follow a trail of never-ending discovery and adventure. You could explore rocks, fossils, landforms, and soil. You might travel to fantastic landscapes and try to find out how they were formed. And maybe someday, your discoveries will be used to teach your fellow earthlings how to take care of this wonderful planet we call home.

Important Dates

1834—John Wesley Powell is born on March 24 in Mount Morris, New York.

1838—Family moves to Jackson County, Ohio

1846—Family moves to South Grove, Wisconsin

1850—Leaves home to attend school in Janesville, Wisconsin

1853—Family moves to Wheaton, Illinois. Attends Illinois Institute

1855—Explores Mississippi River. Meets Emma Dean

1858—Begins teaching in Hennepin, Illinois

1861—Enlists in Union army. Marries Emma Dean

1862—Loses arm in battle

1865—Discharged from Union army

1867—Leads first expedition to the Colorado Territory

1869—Explores Grand Canyon region of the Colorado River

1871—Starts second Colorado River trip. Daughter Mary born

1879—Becomes director of United States Bureau of Ethnology

1881—Becomes director of United States Geological Survey

1888—Establishes irrigation survey

1894—Resigns from USGS

1902—Dies September 23

Glossary

crust: Earth's hard outer layer

decompose: to slowly break down and rot into smaller particles

erosion: the wearing away of rock or soil by wind, water, and other forces

ethnology: the study of different cultures

fossils: the remains of once-living things preserved in rock

geologist: a scientist who studies the earth

glaciers: huge, slowly moving sheets of ice

hardness: a mineral's resistance to being scratched

igneous: a type of rock created when hot, liquid rock cools and hardens

irrigation: carrying water to dry land using ditches or pipes

magma: hot, liquid rock found beneath the earth's surface

metamorphic: a type of rock formed when heat, pressure, or other forces cause changes in rocks

mineral: a natural, solid substance that is not an animal or plant. Minerals make up rocks.

naturalist: a person who studies nature

sedimentary: a type of rock created when layers of sediment—tiny particles of rocks, shells, and plants—are squeezed together for a very long time

sedimentation: a process in which tiny particles of rock, shells, and plants accumulate in layers and are slowly turned to rock

uplift: the upward movement of land masses

Bibliography

Crossette, George, ed. *Selected Prose of John Wesley Powell.* Boston: D. R. Godine, 1970.

Darrah, William Culp. *Powell of the Colorado.* Princeton, N. J.: Princeton University Press, 1951.

*Fraser, Mary Ann. *In Search of the Grand Canyon.* New York: Henry Holt, 1995.

Powell, John Wesley. *The Exploration of the Colorado River and Its Canyons.* 1895. Reprint (original title *Canyons of the Colorado*), New York: Dover Publications, 1961.

Schmidt, Jeremy. *The Grand Canyon National Park.* Boston: Houghton Mifflin, 1993.

Stegner, Wallace. *Beyond the Hundredth Meridian.* Boston: Houghton Mifflin, 1954.

Terrell, John Upton. *The Man Who Rediscovered America: A Biography of John Wesley Powell.* New York: Weybright and Talley, Inc., 1969.

*Asterisk indicates a book for young readers.

The quotation on page 22 is reprinted from William Culp Darrah's *Powell of the Colorado.* The quotation on page 31 is reprinted from John Wesley Powell's *The Exploration of the Colorado River and Its Canyons.*

All photographs appear courtesy of the Utah State Historical Society, used by permission, all rights reserved, except: Portraits collection, U.S. Geological Survey, p. 4; National Anthropological Archives, Smithsonian Institution (photo lot 90-1 #551), p. 39.

Index